C000143358

Rites surrounding Death

The Palermo Statement of the
International Anglican Liturgical
Consultation 2007

Edited with introduction and commentary
by Trevor Lloyd

Member of the Church of England Liturgical Commission 1980–2002

Contents

The cover picture is taken from the Burial service in the 1662 Book of Common Prayer, and is shown in the original manuscript form of the Book Annexed to the 1662 Act of Uniformity which enforced its use, and it is reproduced here from a 19th facsimile copy of the Annexed Book.

First published October 2012
The Statement © the International Anglican Liturgical Consultation
Editorial content and arrangement, including the Commentary ©
Trevor Lloyd 2012

ISSN 0951-2667
ISBN 978-1-84825-323-0

Commendatory Note

by the Chair of the Steering Committee of the International Anglican Liturgical Consultation

I write to commend this Alcuin/GROW Joint Liturgical Study to a worldwide readership. In previous International Consultations, notably at Toronto (1991), Dublin (1995) and Berkeley (2001), finished statements on liturgical matters of central concern within the Anglican Communion have been first issued as Statements, and have then been further reinforced and publicized by a later publication of collected essays accompanying and expounding the Statement. In this case, however, the Statement was in draft form at the end of IALC-8 at Palermo, and so was not then 'signed off' but was referred to the Steering Committee elected at the end of that Consultation. I was a member of that Committee, and we followed a procedure which is outlined by Trevor Lloyd in his Introduction to this Study. While the Steering Committee, which I have chaired since 2009, had optimistically looked for full endorsement by the Consultations in 2009 or 2011, in fact those Consultations not only had no time to spare to study the resultant Statement in depth, but also had a clear sense that the Statement belonged to IALC-8 at Palermo, and could not well be adopted and owned by later Consultations with different membership. Thus the Steering Committee has responded to the offer of a place within the Joint Liturgical Studies series by re-affirming the Statement as originating from Palermo, though without the individual endorsement of all those present at the time. It has been a pleasure then to entrust to Trevor Lloyd to edit this Study, flanking the Statement with Introduction,

Commentary and Appendices. Trevor is uniquely qualified to relate the existing rites around the Communion to the Statement, not only as having himself taken a large part in the detailed tidying of the Statement after Palermo, but also through his well-attested creative work on the *Common Worship* funeral rites of the Church of England and his widely respected contribution giving an overview of the rites of the Communion in 'Funeral rites' in *The Oxford Guide to the Book of Common Prayer*.

So on behalf of the current IALC Steering Committee, I express our thanks to Trevor Lloyd for undertaking this labour, and our hopes that the resultant Study will be of use throughout the Anglican Communion and beyond.

Eileen Scully, Toronto
Chair of the IALC Steering Committee 2009–13

1

Introduction

The International Anglican Liturgical Consultation (IALC) is the official network for liturgy of the Anglican Communion, recognized by the Anglican Consultative Council and the Primates' Meeting. Its primary responsibility in the Communion is to resource and communicate about liturgy on a communion-wide basis. It usually meets twice in each four-year period, one meeting being an interim or preparatory conference, the other being the full Consultation, at which there is usually a wider representation from across the Communion. It has had a distinguished and influential history, producing normative statements on Baptism (The Toronto Statement, IALC 4, 1991) the Eucharist (The Dublin Statement, IALC 5, 1995), Anglican Ordination Rites (The Berkeley Statement, IALC 6, 2001), and Liturgy and Anglican Identity (Prague, 2005). The meeting at Palermo in Sicily from 30 July to 4 August 2007 was a full Consultation, attended by 53 representatives from 17 countries.[1] It spent most of the time on funeral rites and customs.

To help those across the Anglican Communion, and our ecumenical

---

[1] *Anglican Communion Co-ordinator for Liturgy:* Paul Gibson; *Australia*: Ronald Dowling, Boak Jobbins, Albert Mcpherson, Elizabeth Smith, Gillian Varcoe; *Canada:* Bill Crockett, Eileen Scully, Michelle Staples; *Central Africa:* Bernard Malango; *Czech Republic:* David Holeton; *England:* Andrew Barr, Anders Bergquist, Colin Buchanan, Anne Dawtry, Dana Delap, Alec George, Simon Jones, David Kennedy, Trevor Lloyd, Stephen Platten, Phillip Tovey; *Ghana:* John S. Pobee; *Ireland:* Ricky Rountree, Alan Rufli; *Kenya:* Joyce Karuri, Sam Mawiyou; *New Zealand:* George Connor, Te Kitohi Pikaahu; *Japan:* Bartholomew Takeuchi, John Masato Yoshida; *Philippines:* Tomas S. Maddela; *Southern Africa:* Cynthia Botha, Merwyn Castle, Ian Darby, Keith Griffiths, Bruce Jenneker; *Scotland:* Andrew Barr, Darren Mcfarland, Ian Paton, James Milne; *Sudan,* Ezekiel Kondo; *U.S.A.:* Robert Brooks, Jean Campbell, Carol Doran, Lizette Larson-Miller, Ruth Meyers, Clay Morris, Juan Oliver, Juan Quevedo-Bosch, Louis Weil; *Wales:* Raymond Bayley; *West Indies:* Alfred Reid.

partners and friends, in the task of discussing, preparing and revising our funeral rites, this volume contains summaries of the papers presented at the Consultation, the text of the Statement itself, a Commentary aimed at developing some of the themes of the Statement and providing examples from different provinces in the Communion, a summary of principal addresses at the Consultation and a bibliography of material for further reading, prepared by Lizette Larson-Miller.

Methodology

The methodology of the Consultation, which met for five days, was to hear from five speakers during the first two days, and then to work through smaller discussion groups, which met for around eight hours in total, each with a given area of work.

The keynote address was given by John Pobee, on 'Christian Funerals – an African Perspective', and the other speakers were Bartholomew Takeuchi, the former Dean of St. Andrew's Cathedral, Tokyo, on 'Funerals in a Japanese context' ,Te Kitohi Pikaahu, Bishop of Te Tai Tokerau, the Northern Region of the Maori Tikanga in Aotearoa-New Zealand, who spoke on 'Funeral Rites: Culture and Practice', Paul Gibson (former Liturgical Officer for the Anglican Church of Canada and Coordinator for Liturgy for the Anglican Communion) on 'The Anthropological Background of Funeral Rites', and Jean Campbell (Rector of Trinity Church, Fishkill, New York) on 'The Prayer of Funerals'. Brief summaries of the first three are included here at Appendix 1; some of the comments of the last two have been woven into the Commentary at appropriate points. As well as providing a great deal of background material, the effect of these papers was to impress upon the Consultation how very diverse the cultures and customs are within which Anglican churches are working across the world, especially in this area of death and funeral rites.

The aim of the working groups was to produce several paragraphs of text which could be combined into a coherent statement towards the end of the consultation. Time was allowed for drafting and for plenary debates to share the different sections, before agreeing the main outlines and substance of the statement paragraph by paragraph on the last day. The process did not allow sufficient time for eliminating repetitions or smoothing the text, so the Consultation then referred it to an editing group (Cynthia Botha from South Africa, Ruth Meyers and Louis Weil from the United States, and Trevor Lloyd from England). It came back to the Steering Committee of the Consultation before being circulated to all members in time for consideration at the Consultations in Auckland in 2009 and Canterbury in 2011, where, as indicated by Eileen Scully on page 4 above, no further suggestions for change were made.

This volume reflects the glorious diversity of the Churches in the Anglican Communion and the imaginative ways in which they are grappling with the inculturation of the Christian faith in cultures that are sometimes indifferent, hostile or post-Christian. It provides a snapshot of these concerns at one point in time, and is in no way a full discussion of all the different aspects of the church's ministry to the dying and bereaved. Some will find omissions or angles on subjects that are not fully dealt with: there is nothing, for instance on the issue of prayer and the departed, not much on the communion of saints or the eschatology of funeral rites. But there is enough here to provide a useful checklist for churches and provinces to use to evaluate current ministry and liturgical practice, as we continue to learn from one another.

Trevor Lloyd
September 2012

2

The Palermo Statement: Rites surrounding Death

'The end of funeral duties is first to shew that love towards the party deceased which nature requireth; then to do him that honour which is fit both generally for man and particularly for the quality of his person; last of all to testify the care which the Church hath to comfort the living, and the hope which we all have concerning the resurrection of the dead.' (Richard Hooker, *Ecclesiastical Polity*, V, lxxxv, 1597).

Aim of the Publication

This Statement aims to provide principles for Provinces of the Anglican Communion, particularly liturgy committees, which will enable them

- to develop a continuum of rites that will enrich and support the needs of individuals and communities at the different stages of the journey or procession that make up the process of mourning the dead and disposing of their bodies.

3

Commentary[1]

The Aim of the Publication

The members of the Consultation felt it was important to be clear about what kind of document they were producing, and why. Though there was considerable theological expertise within their number, they were not meeting to produce an academic work of either the theology or liturgical history of rites surrounding death. Nor were they going

---

1 In this chapter, direct quotations from the Statement are in italics, and the prayer books of individual provinces are mentioned in full only on the first occasion when they are quoted, with abbreviations (province or country and date) used thereafter. A complete list of these may be found in Appendix 2.

9

- to provide an educational document for those who lead and interpret funeral rites.
- to provide an outline that will enable people to take responsibility for burying their dead.
- to develop the use of appropriate language and symbol in the rites by
- using concrete rather than abstract language
- being counter-cultural, but in language that people can understand, where the prevailing culture runs counter to the Gospel
- ensuring contemporary resonance with the community.

The context within which such rites will be developed and used will include

- an awareness of the cultural exigencies in the Province for which such rites are being developed
- an observance of the universalities of processes surrounding death
- an awareness that such rites will be used in a context of multi-faith, and of uncertain faith.

---

to produce a definitive outline or order, to be copied by all provinces. Each province is different in terms of its history, cultural and secular expectations of these rites, and local custom, whether considered Christian or not. Each province is also autonomous, responsible for developing rites which are consonant with its own history, culture and expectations, and effective in pastoral and missiological terms.

So the tone of this introduction is slightly diffident, conscious of the vast differences which exist on this subject compared with, say, baptism or the eucharist. The radical cultural differences in the Communion were brought home to members in the course of the initial presentations and subsequent discussion, so there is an emphasis here on the need to be aware of local culture in drafting rites. The question of whether cultural demands should be embraced or denied is not dealt with until Section B, the Social Context.

There are, though, some pointers to areas of agreement even if the cultural differences are large. The Statement speaks about provinces developing 'a continuum of rites', making clear that what is under discussion is not simply 'a funeral service' or in 1662 terms 'The Burial Service'. The process from dying to memorial is like a journey, along which the church should offer support at different stages. This theme is taken up and amplified in Section D, on Structure.

A Introduction

All human life ends in death. The personal and ritual ways in which we respond are determined by our social context, by the cultural and liturgical traditions which we inherit, and by our Christian understanding of death, as well as our perception of our own and others' pastoral needs. This is the ground we aim to outline in this Statement.

Our historic Anglican rites and practices are part of the cultural context which we have inherited and within which we work. The 1662 Book of Common Prayer service for the Burial of the Dead is an important part of that inheritance. When we examine that service and its theological and pastoral provision we find:

- it provides a liturgical celebration of death
- the presence of the body is taken for granted
- it was celebrated in community
- there is a strong statement of belief in resurrection (1 Corinthians 15)

A Introduction

What is it that determines the shape and form of the funeral rite? The first paragraph lists some of the factors – social context, traditions, cultural and liturgical, personal theology and pastoral need – which are explored in further sections of the Statement.

The Statement then picks out one of these, the historic position of the 1662 Book of Common Prayer and offers some pointers to its strengths and weaknesses. This is a good example of the way in which the Statement starts pragmatically from where Churches in the Communion are, rather than engaging in a longer or deeper historical or theological analysis. Those who want that will need to look in the bibliography, which will help those involved in the local revision of rites to explore some of the issues further. But the pragmatic, snapshot-like approach of the Statement is very useful in pin-pointing some of those issues and giving some indication of approaches which the Churches in the Communion share.

On the particular point of the function of the 1662 BCP in the Communion, the Statement leaves aside 600 years of history, including the extended rites of the medieval period in the Western Church, which Cranmer truncated in 1552 into two, the office in church and the burial at the grave, to give us the minimalist shape of the rite we have in 1662. It does this because of the fundamental historic place of the 1662 BCP in holding the Communion together and laying the foundation for the local rites derived

11

- it has no prayer for the dead
- the service retained from the mediaeval rites a sense of God's judgment
- it enables an encounter with one's own mortality, for instance in the choice of Psalms
- there is little provision of comfort to mourners
- its social background was small urban and rural communities in a uniform Christian context.

In the 20th century provinces have adapted this basic rite to their own cultures and contemporary experience, finding the 1662 rite to be inadequate because

- one size cannot fit all situations, so the service needs to be capable of more variety

from it. Many provinces still use a funeral rite closely dependent on 1662 (for example Melanesia)[2] or offer it as one option (for example the Church of the Province of the West Indies).[3] The Consultation was well aware of the cultural extremes, from the minimalist needed in Japan to the maximalist experienced in the series of rites in the Maori church in New Zealand. Is there an Anglican 'norm' somewhere between the two, possibly exhibited by such 'western' or 'mainstream' derivatives from 1662 as Canada,[4] Australia,[5] or The Episcopal Church?[6] The Statement seems to be pretty emphatic that there is no norm or model – and certainly not a western-inspired one – apart from that of meeting local cultural needs in a way that is consonant with our Anglican Christian heritage.

2 *A Melanesian English Prayer Book*, revised 1985.
3 Church of the Province of the West Indies, *Book of Common Prayer* 1995 (hereafter CPWI 1995).
4 *The Book of Alternative Services of the Anglican Church of Canada*, 1985, Anglican Book Centre (hereafter Canada 1985).
5 The Anglican Church of Australia, *A Prayer Book for Australia*, Broughton Books, 1995 (hereafter Australia 1995).
6 The Episcopal Church in the United States of America, *Book of Common Prayer*, 1979, *Book of Occasional Services*, 1979 (hereafter US BCP 1979 and US BOS 1979).

- there is an awareness of the greater range of pastoral needs
- these needs have led to the development of staged rites and seeing
- the funeral liturgy as a process

Liturgical research on historical patterns has also contributed to the revision of rites.

The reasons why 1662 is no longer sufficient are listed and show something of what has driven some to more radical revision. Seeing both dying and grieving as a process has led in some places to the development of a series or stages of rites (for example in New Zealand[7] and England). Pastoral needs, like the causes of death, have changed since the 17th century, so Kenya 2002[8] prays about accidents:

O Lord God almighty, author of all knowledge, we thank you that by your everlasting power you enable your people to invent many things including instruments like vehicles and others, that make travelling easy and fast. But Lord we are sad that, many people including our brother here have died from accident involving these vessels. Hear us Lord as we pray that you would instil in all drivers a sense of responsibility over the people they carry; cause them to respect the sanctity of human life and as much as possible seek to protect the lives under their care. And when all this is done, grant us. Lord, your protection on the roads, the air and the sea, so that we may be safeguarded against sudden deaths.

---

7 Church of the Province of New Zealand, *A New Zealand Prayer Book*, Collins, 1989 (hereafter NZ 1989).
8 Anglican Church of Kenya, *Our Modern Services*, 2002, Uzima (hereafter Kenya 2002).

B The Social Context

Humans have always responded ritually to the finitude of their experience. Cultures in every time and place have developed rites which:

1 provide for the disposal of the body of the deceased
2 restructure the life of the community and the family after the death of one of its members
3 help those affected by death to deal with grieving and loss
4 express beliefs about human destiny
5 recognize the individual's contributions during their life here on earth.

In each of these aspects, ideas of the sacred and profane are interwoven as the community attempts to explore the meaning of death.

B The Social Context

This section begins by setting out what a funeral needs to do: Section D explores this further in terms of culture and anthropology. Some provinces have a list like this in the introductions to their rites, and some (for example Ireland 2004,[9] Australia 1995, US BCP 1979 and CW 2000) put it at the beginning of the liturgy:

> We have come here today
> to remember before God our *brother/sister N*;
> to give thanks for *his/her* life;
> to commend *him/her* to God our merciful redeemer and judge;
> to commit *his/her* body to be *buried/cremated*,
> and to comfort one another in our grief. [10]

If the funeral is a 'universal human experience' as the Statement says, how far should what the Church provides be exclusively Christian, and how far should it go along the continuum towards being so assimilated into the local culture that it is no longer discernibly Christian? Nigeria 1996[11] is clear in its opening note:

9 The Church of Ireland, *The Book of Common Prayer,* 2004, Columba (hereafter Ireland 2004).

10 Church of England, *Common Worship: Pastoral Services, 2000* (hereafter CW 2000). Extracts from *Common Worship Pastoral Services* are copyright © The Archbishops' Council 2000, 2005 and are reproduced by permission.

11 Anglican Church of Nigeria 1983, *The Book of Common Prayer of the Church of Nigeria* 1996 (hereafter Nigeria 1983).

Unlike initiation and the eucharist, which are explicitly Christian rites, Christian funerals are the Church's response to a universal human experience. It follows that funeral rites focus inculturation issues sharply and that we should expect a variety of inculturated Christian practices both across the provinces of the Anglican Communion and within them. We encourage provinces to explore the cultures within their area and to take account of various beliefs and practices relating to death as they impinge on funeral rites.

In some provinces, Anglicans encounter a well-developed traditional funerary culture (e.g., Maori or Japanese). In such situations, the Church must decide which practices are consistent with Christian teaching about death and resurrection and so may be incorporated into its funeral rites, and which practices run counter to the Gospel and so must be challenged. For example, traditional Japanese funeral practices avoid or deny death, and Christians must find ways to proclaim the Christian hope of life after death. In contrast, traditional Maori funeral practice

---

This order is to be used for practising Christians. In case of any doubt on the state of the deceased, reference will be made to the Bishop whose decision is final.

And the service begins 'With faith in Jesus Christ, we receive the body of our sister/brother for burial.'

Kenya 2002 is explicit about it:

This Service is not to be used for those who die unbaptized, excommunicated or those who have committed suicide.

But it also provides an Alternative Burial Service, with notes that say

This service may be used for those with a Christian heritage but who die before they are baptized. It may also be used for people of other faiths who at the time of death were interested in joining the Christian faith. It may also be used in situations where the dead person's religious identity, or walk with the Lord cannot be easily ascertained.

And Kenya 2002 further provides an alternative commendation:

Into your hands, O God, we commend our brother N, as into the hands of a faithful creator and most loving Saviour. In your infinite goodness, wisdom and power, work in him the purpose of your perfect will, Through Jesus Christ our Lord. Amen.

has had a strong sense of the sacred during the period of mourning following a death, and much of this traditional practice has been incorporated into Christian rites.

Elsewhere, particularly in 'western' or 'first world' contexts, the surrounding culture has been shaped by Christianity but that dependence is now attenuated. Here, rather than negotiating a relationship between the Gospel and a vibrant traditional culture, it is a case of trying to help the Christian community to reflect on its own understanding of death and associated rituals. In particular the Christian community may seek to challenge some of the aspects of 21st century western society:

• being a consumer society where process is commodified
• the lack of a community story now experienced
• the lack of a clear link between faith and culture.

For some of us, this would involve taking the funeral back from funeral directors and from secular influences, so that the rite might happen in a

---

US BCP 1979's *Burial of one who does not profess the Christian faith* has a very brief committal:

> You only are immortal, the creator and maker of mankind; and we are mortal, formed of the earth, and to earth shall we return. For so did you ordain when you created me, saying, 'You are dust, and to dust you shall return'. All of us go down to the dust; yet even at the grave we make our song: Alleluia, alleluia, alleluia.

Canada 1992's *Burial of One Who Did Not Profess the Christian Faith* includes prayers designed to honour the person without being specifically Christian:

> We pray that nothing truly good
> in this *man's/woman's* life will be lost,
> but will be of benefit to the world;
> that all that was important to *him/her*
> will be respected by those who follow;
> and that everything in which *he/she* was great
> will continue to mean much to us now that *he/she* is dead.
> We ask you that he/she may go on living
> in *his/her* children, his/her family, and *his/her* friends;
> in their hearts and minds,
> in their courage and their consciences.

godly and respectful way. It might also mean disengaging from the family where we are sometimes expected to act as their own private chaplains to conduct the service, instead of being free as a church team to deliver pastoral care and to encourage transition. We affirm that the liturgy is owned by the Christian community as well as by the minister or clergy leading the rites. Where church members own a service book in their homes, and also a hymn book, they are more likely to feel they own the liturgy with the clergy.

The same service includes a prayer which reflects on the death of someone who did not profess the Christian faith and the effect it has on the mourners:

> We pray for ourselves,
> who are severely tested by this death,
> that we do not try to minimize this loss,
> or seek refuge from it in words alone,
> and also that we do not brood over it
> so that it overwhelms us and isolates us from others.

The middle paragraphs of this section reflect the two introductory addresses on funerals in Japanese and Maori culture, and use these to demonstrate general principles of challenging or building on local cultural patterns. The influence of the pattern of extended Maori rites can be clearly seen in NZ 1979. As well as Prayer at the Time of Death, there is Prayer Before a Funeral, which can be used at home or in church or elsewhere, or when the coffin is brought to the church or marae before a funeral – 'or at any other appropriate time'. And the range of the provision for after the funeral is even more extensive, see below in Section D.

The rest of this section discusses the situation in 21st century 'Western' society, where, as Paul Gibson noted in his address on anthropology, funeral rites are in a process of transition, 'in some cases being owned by the family and community rather than by the church'. The Canada 1985 introduction comments on this change: 'The Church gradually took on roles which once had been the inalienable responsibility of the family or tribe, and the secularization of this process... has led to the development of a profession which relieves bereaved families of many burdens but also sometimes functions as a barrier between families and their funeral rites. It is important to note that funerals are the property of neither undertakers nor clergy. They belong to the circle of family and friends of the person who has died, and when that circle is Christian, they find an appropriate setting in the larger Christian fellowship.' The issue of who owns rites of passage – family, community, church or professionals – will be explored in different ways in different cultures, but this section sets out some of the challenges, though it omits one of the basic ones mentioned by Paul Gibson, the problem 'that many people do not have the historic and doctrinal models from which to begin'. This poses a challenge to the church in terms of mission and doctrinal education – which leads us into the next section.

C Christian Understandings of Death and Funerals

The provinces of the Anglican Communion operate within a wide variety of cultures, some of which have a great depth and breadth of traditions around death and commemoration. There is a richness and helpfulness where church rites reflect and are integrated with their cultural settings while being faithful to the Christian theology of death.

In all funerals there is an expression of beliefs about human destiny. Christian funeral rites are bound to express Christian hope in the redemption of humankind, and the making of a new creation in Christ. This will involve a number of doctrinal issues, for instance:

C Christian Understandings of Death and Funerals

'There is a powerful human impulse to deny the reality and finality of death.' So Paul Gibson reminded the Consultation in his address on anthropology. The primitive core of the funeral service stands as a defence against that denial in its rehearsal of the death that has happened and in helping people look to the future, and our funeral liturgies should embody both. Jesus approached his own death with a plea for deliverance and a cry of forsakenness. A Christian understanding of death and funerals will articulate not only the victory of the cross and the hope of the resurrection, but also deeply felt doubt, fear and the sense of abandonment.

The Statement lists the main doctrinal issues which impinge on funeral rites, each of which merits detailed discussion, exploration and meditation, both by those responsible for the revision of funeral rites and also by all involved in funeral and bereavement ministry. Some of these figure in the introductions to funeral services in some provinces. So the Funeral service of the Anglican Church in Thailand[12] – which ends with a 'Closing Fanfare' – begins with an agenda-setting introduction full of theology:

> We come together –
> to mourn a relative
> to honour a departed friend
> and to show sympathy with the bereaved.
> We believe that those who die in Christ
> share eternal life with him.
> Therefore in faith and hope
> we offer our prayer of thanksgiving and trust to God,
> in whose loving care we leave our friend;

12 Anglican Church in Thailand, *A Prayer Book for Thailand*, 1989.

- Creation in the image of God (with both links to incarnational theology and implications for how we treat the body),
- the work of Christ on the cross (with implications for how we deal with the need for forgiveness and the assurance of eternal life)
- the resurrection of the body (with implications not only relating to

---

> we recall the certainty of our own coming death and judgment;
> and we proclaim that Christ is risen,
> that those who believe in him will rise with him,
> and that we are united with them in him.

The list in the Statement begins with *creation*. Words about God as creator come frequently in the words of commendation ('God our creator and redeemer') and in phrases in prayers ('you love everything that you have made') but the theological implications are worked out in two main ways, both mentioned in paragraph 2 below – *There is work to do for the person who has died*: first, in terms of respect for the body and second, in terms of celebrating the humanity of the dead person.

The work of Christ on the cross raises questions about how – if at all – the issue of forgiveness is dealt with. Wales 2008[13] has a set of brief kyrie petitions:

> Lord Jesus, you raise the dead to life in the Spirit.
> Lord, have mercy. **Lord, have mercy.**
> Lord Jesus, you bring pardon and peace to the sinner.
> Christ, have mercy. **Christ, have mercy**
> Lord Jesus, you give light to those in darkness.
> Lord, have mercy. **Lord, have mercy.**

The therapeutic value of this part of the process of letting go of the dead person is clear, but there is also a spiritual task involved. Ireland 2004 and CW 2000 make similar provision, with Ireland 2004 a single set using the traditional words from Ps 25.5,6 ('Call to remembrance, O Lord, your compassion') while CW 2000 with its usual exuberance provides four sets of Kyries to suit different occasions, and a confession within the Eucharistic version of the Funeral:

> God of mercy,
> we acknowledge that we are all sinners.
> We turn from the wrong that we have thought and said and done,
> and are mindful of all that we have failed to do.

---

13 *Proposed Alternative Funeral Rites for the Church in Wales*, 2008 (hereafter Wales 2008).

Christian hope but also for the ways in which we speak about the body after death)

- the communion of saints and the nature of the church (with implications about how we speak of – and pray about – Christian joy, relationships after death, and heaven, as well as the sense of belonging and support in the church on earth)
- divine judgement within the context of God's infinite grace and mercy (with implications for how we find words which realistically express both sides of the nature of God, without either conjuring up pictures of Dante's Inferno or saying that the demands of the Gospel do not matter)
- the consummation of all things in Christ, setting this death and this funeral in an eschatological perspective.

The ways in which these are expressed in each culture may need to borrow terms and symbols from the culture to express them in ways that are clear and accessible.

The resurrection of the body is seen by the statement as having implications about *the ways in which we speak about the body after death.* This is partly about avoiding the kind of language which gives the impression of a disembodied soul wandering around seeking a home.

The communion of saints and the relationships between the church on earth and in heaven is an important and traditional element in funeral liturgy, raising issues about how to speak liturgically about some folk religion ideas about this relationship. New Zealand 1989 has this helpfully non-specific prayer in the service for unveiling a memorial stone:

> Heavenly Father, help us to entrust our loved ones to your care;
> when sorrow darkens our lives,
> teach us to look to you,
> remembering the cloud of witnesses
> by whom we are surrounded.
> Grant that we on earth may share with them
> the rest and peace which you give
> through your Son, our Lord, Jesus Christ.

Mention of divine judgement and Dante's Inferno may cause some to look for places where the balance between judgement and mercy is clearly expressed: the Consultation was clearly not in favour of the kind of inculturation that assures people that everything will turn out alright in the end.

Christian rites will also need to challenge cultural assumptions that are antithetical to Christian teaching.

These Christian beliefs find expression in the tasks of the church in relation to the funeral:

1 *There is work to do for the Gospel.* Funeral rites are important occasions for the proclamation of the paschal mystery of Christ crucified and risen and the hope of the resurrection. Because they are often attended by those who are not Christian or who are nominally Christian but not regular church-goers, the rites provide opportunities to proclaim the Gospel to those whom it is otherwise very hard to reach by more regular liturgical provisions. Yet those within the Christian community also need to hear the Gospel afresh, so that they are reminded of the basis for Christian hope and the

---

This conservative statement of aspects of the Christian faith as they relate to death is taken further in the three headings that follow, each beginning 'There is work to do...' The proclamation of the Gospel is done not simply in the sermon or homily (England's CW 2000 says 'The purpose of the sermon is to proclaim the gospel in the context of the death of this particular person'), but also in the text of the liturgy. So the commendation in CPWI 1995 stresses the opportunity for renewing our faith:

Grant that his/her death may recall to us your victory over death, and be an occasion for us to renew our trust in your Father's love. Give us, we pray, the faith to follow where you have led the way; and where you live and reign...

and Wales 2008 makes it clear at the start of the service:

In the presence of death,
Christians have sure ground for hope and confidence,
and even for joy,
because the Lord Jesus Christ,
who shared our human life and death,
was raised again triumphant
and lives for evermore.
In him his people find eternal life,
and, in this faith,
we put our whole trust in his goodness and mercy.

21

paradox that our healing, life, and salvation are possible because the one who calls us has died. To proclaim the Gospel effectively, it is important to consider both the form and the content of this proclamation in the local cultural situation. How do we proclaim Christ crucified and risen, in ways that grieving people will be able to hear?

2 *There is work to do for the person who has died.* Some of this work is physical: the care and reverent disposal of the person's body. Some of it is narrative: the storytelling about the life of the person who has died. The Christian imperative in relation to the treatment and disposal of the body is that this should be done with honour, because Christian faith in the Incarnation makes the body central to salvation. The body of a Christian is a body which has been washed in baptism and nourished in the eucharist. What it means in practice

---

The last two sentences of this paragraph of the Statement rightly hint at the problem of grieving families being in a fit state to hear the Gospel and the need to find the right way of doing this within the local culture. In her address to the Consultation on Prayer, Jean Campbell said ' A well-planned funeral is one of the most effective evangelistic opportunities in the parish'. This is because funeral liturgies articulate clearly our faith in the overcoming of death in the paschal mystery and the baptismal promise that we are heirs through Christ in life eternal. Funeral liturgies that do that affirm our faith and bring a clear message of the good news of Jesus Christ to those who have not believed.

There is work to do for the person who has died: the motivation both for treating the body with reverence and for honouring the life of the one who has died is seen to come from the doctrines of creation and incarnation, together with the involvement of the person in the Christian community through baptism and eucharist. Washing is both physical and spiritual, a theme picked up, among others, by the Nigeria 1996 commendation:

> Lord Jesus Christ, we commend to you our brother (sister) N....
> who was reborn by water and the Spirit in Holy Baptism

It is curious that the statement has only one brief mention, hidden in the detailed section on the structure of the rite, of sprinkling or other echoes of baptism in relation to funerals. Even more curiously the issue of how and at what point to honour the life of the one who had died hardly gets a mention in the Statement apart from the phrase here 'the storytelling about the life of the person who has died'. This is despite Paul

to treat with respect the body of the deceased may vary widely from culture to culture, so we can expect the basic Christian principle to find diverse practical expression in different parts of the Anglican Communion. It is also important that nothing happens which may appear to deny the reality of bodily death. Furthermore, because all humankind is created in God's image (Gen 1.26–28), the imperative to honour the body applies also to the occasions when the Church's rite is used for the burial of those who are not Christians.

3   *There is work to do for the living, the survivors, the bereaved, the community.* People need pastoral, physical and spiritual care in whatever mixture of emotions they are experiencing. They need help in negotiating both their actual and their culturally-expected

---

Gibson urging the importance of the human dimension, Te Kitohi Pikaahu's descriptions of long farewell addresses in the Maori tradition, and the evidence from around the Communion that Provinces are making provision for tributes at an early point in the service, for example in Ireland 2004 ('An appropriate place for any tribute... is before the penitential Kyries'), Kenya 2002 ('Eulogies should be well organized and strictly controlled') and CW 2000, which encourages 'remembering and honouring the life of the person who has died' in the earlier part of the service, and provides for it to be done in conjunction with placing symbols of the person's life and faith, with family members or friends taking part.

This section also mentions the danger of appearing *to deny the reality of bodily death.* As we have seen, this is one of the problems the Church faces in Japanese culture, and perhaps 'the reality of death' ought to have been listed under the doctrinal foundations at the start of this section. Such a denial hinders the process of grieving, and this is the focus of the next section, *There is work to do for the living, the survivors, the bereaved, the community.*

The Statement says on page 24 'ways of helping people through grief and loss .... may rightly be incorporated into local Christian liturgies', and there is evidence that this is happening in varying degrees in most provinces. Sometimes this can be found in the introductions. That in Canada 1985 deals with the subject at length: 'Faith is not only belief: faith embraces even its own shadow, which is doubt. Liturgical expressions of faith and hope in the face of death should consequently leave room for the radical sense of anxiety and loss which the mourners experience. They should also enable, rather than deny, the grief process...' NZ 1979 and CW 2000 have a half page of pastoral introduction for the congregation to read before the service, acknowledging grief and responsibilities and needs. Liturgical rites always have a pastoral dimension, though clearly, not all the pastoral work can or should be done in the course of the rites. Ways of helping people through grief and loss are embedded in many local cultures, and may rightly be incorporated into local Christian liturgies. Provinces might find it stimulating to discover and draw upon those practices which Provinces in other cultures find profitable. At the same time, such practices must always serve the function of relating the individual's and community's journey to the Gospel paradigm of the paschal mystery of Christ's death and resurrection and our participation therein.

the part the service plays in the process: 'Grief is like a wound which requires time and care if it is to heal' (NZ 1979). US BCP 1979 has a Note: 'The liturgy for the dead is an Easter liturgy. It finds all its meaning in the resurrection. Because Jesus was raised from the dead, we, too, shall be raised. The liturgy, therefore is characterized by joy... This joy, however, does not make human grief unchristian. The very love we have for each other brings deep sorrow when we are parted by death...'. And there are texts within the liturgy which pick up the theme of grieving, as these examples show:

Father,
You know our hearts and share our sorrows.
We are hurt by our parting
from N. whom we loved:
When we are angry at the loss we have sustained,
when we long for words of comfort,
yet find them hard to hear,
turn our grief to truer living,
our affliction to firmer hope
and our sorrow to deeper joy. (Scotland 1987[14])

Loving God, we come in shock and sadness.
By grace and power you gave us opportunity
to create new life;
now we feel our human frailty.
Hear our cries of disappointment and anger
because of the loss of this new life.
Be with us as we struggle
to understand the mystery of life and death. (Canada 1992, After a
    Miscarriage or a Stillbirth)

---

14 Scottish Episcopal Church, *Revised Funeral Rites*, 1987 (hereafter Scotland 1987).

Funeral rites are important not only to individuals but to the community. In societies where the sense of community is strong, funeral rites are an important way in which community relations are redefined after the dislocation caused by a death. Where the concept and experience of community have become weak, funeral rites provide an opportunity for the church to strengthen a sense of community. A baptismal ecclesiology, which holds that all the

---

We confess that we are slow to accept death
as an inevitable part of life,
We confess our reluctance to surrender N, our friend and loved one,
    into your eternal care (Australia 1995)

in our grief and shock contain and comfort us
embrace us with your love,
give us hope in our confusion
and grace to let go into new life; (CW 2000)

we also remember times when it was hard for us to understand,
to forgive, and to be forgiven.
Heal our memories of hurt and failure,
and bring us to forgiveness and life. (CW 2000)

As Jean Campbell put it. 'The many faces of human mourning have compelled us to provide multiple prayers expressing human grief and mourning.'

This section ends with a paragraph about the importance of the funeral to the community. This may involve very practical considerations, as in Kenya, where funerals can bring impoverishment to the family, so Kenya 2002 has two Notes:

The Synod of the Anglican Church of Kenya has advised that the whole burial service should not exceed two hours; feeding should be very minimal. if any.

A simple and inexpensive burial is advised: burial ceremonies should not overtake the resources of the bereaved.

members of Christ's body are empowered by the Holy Spirit to share in Christ's ministry of care, reinforces the need for the participation of many members of the Christian community in the care of the dying and of the bereaved. Whether the sense of community is strong or weak, Christians will also seek to enlarge the experience of community by affirming both the reality of the Communion of Saints and the Christian belief that through death human life is changed and not taken away.

The ways in which the community is involved will vary from culture to culture, often within provinces. This paragraph provides a useful stimulant (or checklist) for churches wishing to evaluate their ministry to the bereaved: who is involved, and why? CW 2000 is one of the places which specifically says that some of the ancillary rites may well be led by lay people.

The community dimension is of course not limited to the Christian community on earth, and the sense of the immediacy of heaven, with its inhabitants, is not a distant hope in a Christian funeral. ACSA 1989[15] expresses this:

Eternal God and Father
whose love is stronger than death
we rejoice that the dead as well as the living
are in your love and care;
and as we remember with thanksgiving N
and all those who have gone before us
in the way of Christ
we pray that we may be counted worthy
to share with them the life of your kingdom;
through Jesus Christ our Lord. **Amen.**

---

15 The Anglican Church of Southern Africa *An Anglican Prayer Book*, 1989 (henceforth ACSA 1989).

D Structure

The image of 'journey' is very helpful in understanding funeral rites, and many recent revisions of funeral rites around the Anglican Communion have consciously understood the rites as journeys. These are part of our universal human experience of death. There is the journey both physical and spiritual of the person who has died. There is also the journey of the bereaved through the time approaching death, through preparation for the funeral and disposal of the body, towards gradual reintegration into ongoing community life.

The journey

- includes elements of separation, transition and re-incorporation
- starts with those gathered at the site of one who has died or is close to death.
- involves the movement of the body from the point of death to the place of disposal.

D Structure

In his address on the anthropological background Paul Gibson suggested that the funeral was possibly 'the primal religious rite' and noted that 'the fundamental and recurring action' of moving the body from the dwelling to the place of burial, exposure or cremation, followed by the return of the bearers, 'secured the place of the procession as the basic module of the Christian rite'. This is reflected in the Johannine Easter story, full of processions to and from the tomb. Sharing this basic structure – as the Statement says 'part of our universal human experience of death' – should make it easier for us to relate to the local culture, whether Christian or not.

The statement underlines the importance of seeing the funeral as a unitary rite, even though it may be broken up into a series of stages and events in different places. A number of provinces have developed flexible structures for funeral rites. CSI[16] has a 'Common Liturgical Section', with sections for the burial of an adult, a child, youngsters and the 'suicided'. CW 2000's Outline Orders – for both adult and child funerals and

---

16 Church of South India, *Book of Common Worship*, 2006, CSI Centre, Chennai. (hereafter CSI 2006).

The basic elements of this process are pre-Christian. Fundamentally, a funeral accomplishes the disposal of a body in a culturally appropriate way. A Christian funeral acknowledges the paradox of grief and hope, death and resurrection, lament and rejoicing. Not all members of the community will be present in all phases of the rite, so recapitulation of elements of the rite may be appropriate at different stages.

The funeral is a unitary rite, though it may take place in more than one place, and be extended in time. Particular sensitivity needs to be exercised with regard to the position of the committal. Ideally someone should accompany the body throughout the whole of its journey. This is especially relevant in those cultures where cremation is practised.

Pre-funeral rites

A variety of pre-funeral rites may be appropriate, for example, prayers at the time of death, prayers in the home, prayers and rituals at the preparation of the body, receiving the body in the church prior to the order of funeral rites. In some places, vigil liturgies precede the official funeral rites, while in other places they are part of the order of funeral rites. Provinces should develop these rites as they see appropriate. Such

---

for a memorial Service – are designed to encourage flexibility, and a note demonstrates the same thing:
The Committal is used at the point at which it is needed, for example:

- at the burial of the body in a cemetery or churchyard,
- at the interment of ashes when this follows on the same day
- or the day following cremation, in which case the second 'preparation for burial' prayer (page 269) is used at the crematorium, or
- at a crematorium when the interment of ashes is not to follow immediately.

and also provides words for burial in a vault, another cultural variation.

Pre-funeral rites. The list here provides simply a number of examples. Ministry at the Time of Death can be found in CW 2000, ACSA 1989, NZ 1979, and prayers in the home before the funeral are provided in CSI 2006, Canada 1985, NZ 1979, CW 2000.

rites may link people's natural religiosity and social customs with ecclesial rites. In this way both religiosity and social customs might be informed and infused with the Christian gospel.

The funeral rite

The structure of the rite parallels other Christian rites. The elements include:

Gathering of the community which may have taken place over time, in the home, at the funeral parlour or before the commencement of the service in the church.

CW 2000 has a very rich provision for a vigil, on a series of different themes, Assurance and Comfort, The Hope of heaven, An Unexpected Death, with readings, canticles, psalms and psalm prayers, for example:

> Our eyes, Lord, are wasted with grief;
> you know we are weary with groaning.
> As we remember our death
> in the dark emptiness of the night,

Scotland 1987 has

Prayer at the closing of the coffin

> Father,
> your servant's eyes have closed
> in the final sleep of death,
> eyes that laughed, eyes that shed tears.
> Let them wake to the full vision of your glory,
> and our brother/sister see you face to face;
> through Jesus Christ our Lord. **Amen.**

The funeral rite. The *Gathering of the community* is important, because it recognizes at the beginning of the service the place of the community, as discussed at the end of the previous section. Each death brings changes and transformation to the community. It is also the place to recognize that the community gathered for the funeral is composed of many and different communities who have related to the dead person in different

The liturgy of the word consists of appropriate biblical and (optionally) non-biblical readings and a homily which proclaims the gospel of hope. In some rites eulogies and tributes occur as part of the gathering. Wherever it is placed in the service, the homily needs to make the connection between the narratives of the deceased's life and the narrative of God's mighty acts in Christ.

---

ways – part of the art of leading the service is to gather these into one. Scotland 1987 puts this well in the Introduction:

> Bereavement presents an opportunity for pastoral care at three different levels. First there is the ministry to those who are directly involved.
> Secondly there are many people who attend a funeral with little or no church connection, but, at a moment of some significance, may be helped or challenged by what the Gospel has to say about death and eternal life.
> Third, a funeral service is a statement to the whole of our society of the way in which the Christian faith gives meaning to life and to its conclusion in death.

Yet the majority of services in the Communion follow 1662 in going straight into the service, and a 'gathering' text – despite the long-standing obvious parallel with 'We are gathered here in the sight of God...' in the marriage service – is still fairly rare in Anglican liturgies, though it may be found in Ireland 2004, Australia 1995, NZ 1989 and CW 2000:

> We have come here today
> to remember before God our brother/sister N;
> to give thanks for his/her life;
> to commend him/her to God our merciful redeemer and judge;
> to commit his/her body to be buried/cremated,
> and to comfort one another in our grief. (CW 2000)

The liturgy of the word in some places is very open in allowing non-biblical readings; in others, it is prescriptive, like this description of the sermon in Australia 1995:

> *The sermon* should contain at least some of the following:
> (a) proclamation of the Christian hope – Christ crucified and risen;
> (b) acknowledgement of the *reality* of suffering, and that God in Christ has embraced it;
> (c) sensitive concern for the bereaved;
> (d) thanksgiving to God for the life of the deceased; and
> (e) some reminder of our own coming death and judgment.

Prayers follow, typically prayers of thanksgiving, prayers for those who mourn, and prayer for faith. It is important to maintain a balance

Prayers: the Statement here itemizes three areas for prayer – thanksgiving, the bereaved and prayer for faith. Most rites allow for a series of separate prayers, some (like CW 2000 or Australia 1995) with an extensive collection from which to choose. But there are also litanies: CW 2000's four paragraph provision recognizes the difficulty of expecting some funeral congregations to make the responses and puts them in brackets. Scotland 1987 provides sections covering different needs which can be inserted, such as this one for *sorrow, guilt and regret*:

> Forgiving God,
> in the face of death we discover
> how many things are still undone,
> how much might have been done otherwise.
> Redeem our failure.
> Bind up the wounds of past mistakes.
> Transform our guilt to active love,
> and by your forgiveness make us whole.
> Lord, in your mercy...

The theme of thanksgiving is only lightly touched on here, but takes two forms, demonstrated from the section on Thanksgivings in Ireland 2004. First, thanksgiving for the life of the one who has died:

> Heavenly Father,
> we thank you for your servant....;
> for the example he/she has left us,
> and for the fellowship we have enjoyed with him/her.

And second, the kind of eschatological thanksgiving – sometimes developed from the first, that takes us to the heavenly banquet:

> Eternal God, we give thanks
> for all those who have died in faith,
> for the unceasing praise of the company of heaven,
> for the promise to those who mourn
> that all tears shall be wiped away,
> for the pledge of death destroyed and victory won,
> for our foretaste of eternal life
> through baptism and eucharist,
> for our hope in the Spirit,
> for the communion of saints.
> May we live by faith, walk in hope and be renewed in love,
> until the world reflects your glory
> and you are all in all.
> Even so, come, Lord Jesus. Amen.

31

between personal reference and connection with the wider community. Opportunity for the community to celebrate the *eucharist* should be offered. It is appropriate for the deceased person's name to be mentioned in the context of the thanksgiving as a way of making connection with the idea of the communion of saints.

The commendation is pivotal. Here we commend the deceased by name to God's keeping, and affirm our trust in Christ's power over death and

---

ACSA 1989 provides a litany to conclude the prayers, with a response focussed on faith:

> Father, we come to you in our grief, trusting in your love for N and for ourselves. We know that death cannot separate us from your love in Jesus Christ our Lord.
> This is our faith
> **Lord, increase our faith**
> Father, your Son Jesus wept at the tomb of Lazarus We believe that you share our grief and will give strength in our loss.
> This is our faith
> **Lord, increase our faith**
> Father, Jesus died that we might be forgiven. We trust in your forgiveness for N and for ourselves.
> This is our faith
> **Lord, increase our faith**
> Father, you gave your only Son, that all who have faith in him may not die, but have eternal life.
> This is the faith of the Church
> **This is our faith Amen. Alleluia**

The commendation usually takes a fairly standard form, but nuances can be observed of the balance between judgment and love, as in this commendation from NZ 1979:

> God alone is holy and just and good.
> In that confidence, therefore,
> we commend you, N,
> to God's judgement and mercy,
> to God's forgiveness and love.
> Blessed be God the Father,
> who has caused the light of Christ
> to shine upon you.

in the hope of resurrection. The commendation is a discrete unit, not something added to the prayers or incorporated into the dismissal.

Go forth from this world:
in the love of God the Father
who created you,
in the mercy of Jesus Christ
who redeemed you,
in the power of the Holy Spirit
who strengthens you.
In communion with all the faithful,
may you dwell this day in peace.

Sometimes the theology in the Commendation is rich, as in this one from CW 2000, rehearsing the story of redemption:

Almighty God,
in your great love
you crafted us by your hand
and breathed life into us by your Spirit.
Although we became a rebellious people,
you did not abandon us to our sin.
In your tender mercy
you sent your Son
to restore in us your image.
In obedience to your will
he gave up his life for us,
bearing in his body our sins on the cross.
By your mighty power
you raised him from the grave
and exalted him to the throne of glory.
Rejoicing in his victory
and trusting in your promise
to make alive all who turn to Christ,
we commend N to your mercy
and we join with all your faithful people
and the whole company of heaven
in the one unending song of praise:
glory and wisdom and honour
be to our God for ever and ever.

The *committal* is an integral part of the liturgy, taking place at the burial or cremation.

The *dismissal* at the end of a liturgy in church may appropriately suggest the next stage of the journey, for example, the Roman rite's 'In peace let us take our brother/sister N to his/her place of rest.'

The underlying action of the funeral is procession. Wherever possible, the body should be accompanied by representatives of the community, who should be given the opportunity to 'do things for the deceased'. In many cultures, a disconnection has arisen between the community and the deceased, with professionals taking over many acts such as the preparation of the body and its transport. Symbolic acts are important:

The *committal* words often follow a pattern that begins with 'Now, therefore…', linking it to the Commendation. One of the NZ 1979 options is more definite – and down to earth – about death:

Since the earthly life of N
has come to an end,
we commit her/his body to be buried / turned to ashes;

The Statement offers no help over the words to be used at a crematorium or funeral pyre. NZ 1979's 'to be turned to ashes' sounds genteel compared with CNI 1995 'to be burned'. Many (ACSA 1989, Australia 1995) settle for 'to be cremated'. In Kenya 2002 the committal is almost incidental to what is going on in heaven: 'we give the spirit of our brother here departed into the everlasting arms of God to take him to himself, while we commit his body to the ground: Earth to earth…For all the redeemed of the Lord, our sure hope is in the resurrection to eternal life through Jesus Christ, our Lord, who shall change….', followed by verses from Revelation 7. Only CW 2000 makes the point that committal is into the ground, with cremation being preparatory for that: 'now, in preparation for burial, we give his/her body to be cremated.'

This section also includes another comment (see the end of section B, *The Social Context*) about the danger of professionals taking over elements of the funeral: here the concern, at this stage in the service, is about transport, hence the comment that it is best if the body is *accompanied by representatives of the community*. Symbolic acts and music are also considered, all too briefly, and provinces will probably wish to have more detailed discussion on these in relation to the local culture before offering guidance. The Canada 1985 Introduction again relates this to the question of who 'owns' the funeral.

e.g. the placing of tokens of a person's life, the use of water to recall baptism, getting dirty hands at the graveside.

Music enables the expression of many of the theological and psychological elements of the funeral. Hymns proclaim faith, express grief, and carry memory of the person who has died.

Rites after the funeral

After the funeral it may be appropriate that there be a series of rites, for example, the later interment of ashes or bones, memorial services, Eucharists at regularly scheduled intervals (such as the third or seventh day), rites associated with the first anniversary, a dedication of a memorial, the inclusion of the dead in the Sunday intercessions, and

---

Rites after the funeral. Many churches have moved on from simply providing a service for the burial of ashes. ACSA provided in its 1989 *Prayer Book* a Memorial Service and Dedication and Unveiling of a Tombstone, but it has added, in its 2008 *Worship Resource* file Committal of Bodies handed over to Science, The End of the Period of Mourning, and Reburial after Exhumation. Following Maori custom, NZ 1989 has Prayers in a House after Death marking the family's return home after the funeral, with a meal and the re-hallowing of the house for the now smaller family. A year later, The Unveiling of a Memorial symbolizes a new beginning. CW 2000 has At Home after the Funeral:

> Almighty God, the Father of our Lord Jesus Christ,
> whose disciples recognized him as he broke bread
> at their table after the resurrection:
> we thank you for your strength upholding us
> in what we have done today,
> and now we ask for your presence to be recognized in this home;

annual commemorative liturgies around All Saintstide. These practices express the rich Christian theology of remembrance and thankfulness which include human remembrance, the remembrance of God and our ongoing relationship in Christ beyond death.

Memorial Services In some cultures, memorial services are tending to supersede funerals and, in response to secular pressures, may have the effect of 'squeezing out God'. Here too it is important to connect the narratives of the dead person with the acts of God. In all these rites it is essential that the theological thrust of the core rite be reflected, particularly the focus on the death of a Christian in, through and with the death and resurrection of Christ.

Memorial services may need to be far more flexible and tailored to the individual who has died, but the Statement is clear in its warning that this should not lead to a dilution of the Christian content. CW 2000 has an outline Order, which helps to safeguard this. The content should stand closer to that of the funeral service than to a set of reminiscences. CNI[17] expects ministers to use The Burial of the Dead[18] 'as a source book for Memorial Services and other occasions connected with a burial'.

---

17 Church of North India, *The Book of Worship*, ISPCK 1995.
18 Despite the title, the service has 'the committal of the body to the earth, or to be burned, or to the sea'.

E Pastoral Issues

The pastoral issues raised by funerals vary so widely because of our different cultures and local traditions that it is impossible to do more than indicate some general principles. What follows might be summarized as 'listen before you speak'!

1. *Listen* to the cultures of the place and the people, and understand what is 'traditional', 'normal', 'fashionable', 'expected' about rituals surrounding death. This includes not only explicitly religious rituals but also prevailing customs and habits.

2. *Listen* to the anxieties, hopes and religious beliefs (however expressed) of the bereaved. Search especially for points of contact and conflict with both the culture and the Gospel.

E Pastoral Issues

This section majors on the need to listen, to be aware, before speaking. Reflecting on who is present, perhaps along the lines of the Introduction from Scotland 1987 quoted above at the Gathering, will aid that listening. Some may have travelled long distances, reflected in this prayer from Nigeria 1996:

> O Lord, be merciful to all travellers especially those
> who have travelled from far and near places
> to commiserate with the bereaved,
> and grant them a safe return,
> bless, guide and defend them,
> protect them from perils and dangers of the road
> prosper them in their course,
> that they, beholding your mercy.
> and praising you for your goodness here.
> May they more be quickened with a desire
> for the full enjoyment of their privileges
> as fellow-citizens with the saints in your heavenly household,
> through Jesus Christ, our Lord. **Amen.**

3. *Be aware of* – and make provision for – the way in which both the local culture and the Gospel make provision for the fact that death occurs in a variety of circumstances, some of which present issues for the whole Church family: for example, the death of a child or teenager, death by suicide, sudden death (drug overdose, violent death), neonatal death and stillbirth. In addition, the modern reality of withdrawal of life support raises particular concerns. These situations call for a variety of resources from which ministers might select appropriate material to fit into the funeral structure. In the case of the death of a child a distinct rite may be composed, following the structure outlined above; alternatively a selection of prayers, of thanksgiving for life, for the parents, and for caregivers might be made available.

4 *Speak and enact* the Gospel as Good News hearable in the language and embodied in the patterns of these particular people. There will be times when a critique of the culturally held values or beliefs must be

---

For many, anxiety will be triggered by a reminder of the uncertainty of life, as in this CSI 2006 prayer 'At the Burial of Youngsters'

> Eternal God, we acknowledge the uncertainty of our life on earth. We are given a mere handful of days, and our span of life seems nothing in your sight. All flesh is as grass; and all its beauty is like the flower of the field. The grass withers, the flower fades; but your word will stand forever. In this is our hope, for you are our God. Even in the valley of the shadow of death, you are with us. O Lord, let us know our end and the number of our days, that we may learn how fleeting life is. Turn your ear to our cry, and hear our prayer. Do not be silent at our tears, for we live as strangers before you, wandering pilgrims as all our ancestors were. But you are the same and your years shall have no end. **Amen**

This section lists a wide variety of other funeral situations for which Provinces have provided either prayers or complete services, such as that quoted above. In her address on Prayer at the beginning of the Consultation, Jean Campbell noted that CW 2000 includes a selection of prayers which correspond to various kinds of grief and pointed to the US 2007 *Enriching our Worship* prayers about miscarriage and the withdrawal of medical treatment for the terminally ill. She thought we were also beginning to recognize the need to affirm lament.

offered from the Christian perspective. There will be other times when locally held beliefs and hopes can be wholeheartedly affirmed in terms of Christian faith.

No set of texts or rubrics, however comprehensive or permissive, can do all this without the mediation of pastorally sensitive, theologically astute and liturgically fluent clergy. However, liturgical theologians have special responsibilities in the process. They must assist especially in attending to and offering critique and affirmation of the cultures; in articulating the emotions of the community which may include fear, anger, stigma, and guilt; and in translating the Christian Good News into culturally appropriate, theologically rich and ritually effective forms.

F Conclusion

Some Provinces have already published rites addressing the issues presented above. We commend further study and sharing of these rites. Electronic publication makes mutual learning and adaptation possible. Also we encourage Provinces to produce materials for study and use in their own diocesan and cultural contexts, including local compositions, and to investigate ways of sharing these with others, for example through the Liaison Officer for Liturgy for the Anglican Communion.

The last paragraph in this section might well have come in the conclusion, calling for *pastorally sensitive, theologically astute and liturgically fluent clergy* supported by liturgical theologians who know how to articulate the emotions of the community as well as the Gospel. The Statement just about avoids making an appeal for the resources to provide education and training for all of this, as well as for the use of electronic media and the research and co-ordination role of the Anglican Communion's Liaison Officer for Liturgy. Clearly more resources would help, at every level, both nationally and internationally, but the evidence, in the Statement and in the texts that are available, is that this area of the Communion's ministry is alive and well, meeting the varied needs of many thousands of people.

Appendix 1

Summary of Addresses

Africa

The keynote address was given by John Pobee, on 'Christian Funerals – an African Perspective'. Born into a Ghanaian family, John studied at the University of Ghana, Selwyn College, Cambridge and Westcott House, Cambridge. He was Head of Department for the Study of Religions, and Dean of the Faculty of Arts at the University of Ghana, He later worked at the World Council of Churches in Geneva. He reminded the meeting that we have an immoveable feast – death. Whatever we do includes the element of transition, of going and moving somewhere. All of life is punctuated by crisis points, of which death is one. We tend to isolate death, but we should see it as part of a series of events which happen at intervals in our lives: it is not necessarily morbid, but part of life. As a rite of transition, or rite of passage, death includes the three elements of separation, transition, and incorporation. Incorporation was important in the African context because of the sense of community. We are only able to make sense of things within a sense of community. The funeral rite contributes to that, with the community being renewed by people coming together. In Africa, if someone does not go to funerals their community may not allow them to bury their own relations in the community burial place. In Ghana it is hard to get people to work on Fridays, because they are busy going to funerals and burials. Funerals provide a sense of solidarity.

In all this, the liturgy is important. 'Liturgy is about communication, and it is useless if it fails to communicate with the emotions.' It is important that liturgy be beautiful, but a sense of beauty is now in a confused state. We also need a sense of colour. He said he thought we could do something with colour in our community. The colours at a funeral tell the story. We must ask what message does this colour have in a particular context? For his culture, drama and symbolism were very important, but symbols could not easily be translated from one culture to another. He ended by asking, 'What ideas do I want to communicate through the funeral service?' and listed three. First, death is the necessary and unavoidable destiny for all of us. Second, faith in Jesus Christ makes a difference. How different is my funeral as a Christian? Third, life everlasting and the communion of saints is an important dimension, including in the community those who have gone before.

Japan

Bartholomew Takeuchi, the former Dean of St Andrew's Cathedral, Tokyo, described 'Funerals in a Japanese Context'. He outlined some of the history of the Japanese church following the decision of the Japanese government in 1868 to open the country to the western world, after centuries of persecution during which Christianity had been forbidden and 200,000 martyrs had died, more than in the Roman persecution of the early church. Christianity came back to Japan in 1859 in the person of Channing Moor Williams, a missionary from the American Episcopal Church. But the missionaries to Japan came simply to increase the number of Christians, measuring their success in terms of the number of the newly-baptized, and there was practically no evidence of liturgical activity. For the first 15 years or so the Japanese church did only morning and evening prayers. The Nippon Sei Ko Kai ('The Holy Church of Japan', as the Anglican Episcopal Church is known) was established in 1888 when its first convention was held. The Church of England sent missionaries from two societies and the Americans from one, and all three maintained their own churches. They then started to divide Japan into ten areas for which the societies were respectively responsible. Liturgical matters were affected by the practice of the three different bodies. Bishops in the NSKK have been working very hard for the unity of the Japanese church for a long time.

When you look at Japanese society there is another big problem. After 150 years in Japan, statistics show that the Christian population is less than 1 per cent out of 120,000,000. There are probably 30,000 members of the NSKK. The majority of the Japanese people are not Christians but they are not persecutors. They are simply different or indifferent to a Christian religion, and more or less to other religions, too. Religion has been treated as a means of government since the seventeenth century. Most of the Japanese people don't see any value or teaching that they want to follow in any sort of religion. They try to follow what their ancestors taught them, about how to live with earthly happiness. Living or living on this earth is the highest value among the Japanese people. In turn, therefore, death is the reality they do not accept.

Graves are the tokens that someone still lives. So there is pressure on the family to keep the graves in a proper way; it is the highest and most important obligation for everyone. Bartholomew told of a young woman who wanted to marry a young man whose family objected because she was a Christian. They thought a Christian would never keep the graves in the proper way. Japanese people thought Christianity was about love and helping others and perhaps against drinking and smoking. Ordinary people thought that Christianity was a long way from keeping the graves in a proper way. The task of missionaries was concentrated on expansion. The Japanese government wanted to modernize Japan and sometimes tried to use the missionaries as promoters of western culture. Christianity was regarded not as a system of faith or a way of life but as a kind of expression of European or American culture. The west was always better, so they tried to receive western values into every corner of their lives. Chinese Christians have criticized the Japanese church for its role in westernization. Japanese people still think that Christianity is an expression of a sort of superiority and modernization. For the Japanese, 'new' means 'good' or 'better'. When a baby is born, people go to Shinto shrines to report to the ancestors. When there is a marriage, some may go to the Shinto shrine for a wedding tea, but more often people go to a church, because it is an expression of Western culture, with Western music and fashionable dress. But when someone dies, people go to a Buddhist temple. That emphasizes peace and hope for the future, because the dead person is still alive.

Japanese people never accept death. A dead person is still there, but people don't want to accept the reality of death. They think that the dead still see the living, with a strong sense of jealousy. The regrets of the dead become a grudge against the living. If the living are unkind or forgetful, the dead may bring a curse on the family. So there are rituals to say 'please go away peacefully' and 'We will remember you but please don't remember us.' This kind of thinking does not come from Buddhism. When the Buddhists came in the sixth century, they transformed Japanese folk religion into a Japanese version of Buddhism. Before the sixth century, there was no distinction between life and death; death was not accepted, and there was no distinction between this world and that world. The folk religion shows only a kind of river that divides this world and that world. In Buddhism, the highest value for humanity is nothingness, but in this powerful folk religion the highest value is going on living and being part of the life of the family, so the rituals are all about satisfying the dead and getting them to give up their life and go away.

The main Buddhist practice at the time of death gives opportunity for the survivors to say, 'Please go away without leaving any curse upon us.' The Sanskrit scriptures celebrating nothingness are read at great length all through the night. This is 'TSUYA' (literally 'all through the night'), the vigil for the dead. In *tsuya* services, the survived wish the dead one to leave this world and try to convince the dead one that he/she shall be remembered with utmost respect and gratitude so that the dead one would be satisfied and be able to face his/her death without any grudge. At *tsuya*, which tends to be a great gathering, people are entertained with some good food and drinks that are supposed to be a great banquet provided by the dead one. The quality and quantity of food and drinks show the people the dead one's generosity. Because of this *tsuya*, the funeral service itself becomes not so important but is a kind of public or official announcement of the change in this person's life. More important is to repeat this kind of memorial seven times and let the dead one go. On the 49th day the process is supposed to be successfully completed and the dead one has gone with some satisfaction and a sense of giving up and will not put a curse on the living.

Then cremation comes, which has been a matter of law in Japan since the Spanish flu killed thousands in the early twentieth century. The bones which remain after cremation are of great importance. But this is not a Buddhist custom because the doctrine of nothingness has nothing to do with the bones. The bones are the only evidence of the person's existence, and many people wish to keep the cremated bones, not ashes, in their homes as long as possible. For Christians the bones are not so important, which perplexes Japanese people.

The rituals are a real problem for Christians, because people expect Christians to do the same as everyone else, and they are usually a tiny minority. Sometimes the dead person is the only member of his/her family who was a Christian. Even church people think almost in the same way as non-Christian Japanese. And sometimes, people demand that even the church should follow the ways customarily done in the society, however different from the Christian understanding of death. This is a great problem for pastoral ministry. The NSKK has endeavoured to produce in the form of the official prayer book ways of giving Japanese traditional ideas about death and the rituals around death a new understanding according to a Christian theology of death.

Aotearoa-New Zealand

Te Kitohi Pikaahu, Bishop of Te Tai Tokerau, the Northern Region of the Maori Tikanga, spoke on 'Funeral Rites: Culture and Practice' from the perspective of a Maori world view. He began with a short whakatauki-proverb that refers to death and life: When one fern frond dies a new frond emerges. When one warrior dies another one takes his place. In life we are in death, and in death we are in life. In looking at funeral rites from Aotearoa-New Zealand it is important to note that the whole New Zealand church had been influenced by Maori funeral rites and that the church as a whole has embraced Maori practices now absorbed fully in its liturgy in both languages. He quoted a New Zealand church leader, who expressed the opinion that the way toward understanding the Maori world view is only possible through a subjective approach. Trying to understand Maori thought, custom and experience through abstract means will lead only to a dead end. Maori culture is very rich in mythology and tradition, much of it still preserved as passed down from generation to generation in spite of some adaptation and natural evolution to suit the context, time, and location. These traditions still play a significant role in Maori life.

As an example Te Kitohi Pikaahu referred to the large and public funeral for the Maori Queen, Dame Te Ata-i-rangi-kaahu which was televised. The mourning process was covered by the media. This brought the richness of Maori ritual at its best to every home and reinforced pride in being and behaving as a Maori.

Ritual surrounding death has remained more or less intact among traditional Maori, revealing Maori perceptions of the soul and the afterlife. The Maori concept of death is that the spirit of the deceased goes to the spirit world, joining the ancestors, and is always within the realm of Maori daily life and experience. The past, present, and future are intricately connected through memory and story.

There are three stages in the rites related to death: a preparation phase centred on the individual, a gathering phase centred on the community, and a post-funeral phase centred on the immediate family. Te Kitohi Pikaahu took the Consultation through some of the components of the mourning process: mourning (lament), the provision of time for the rituals to take place, the sacred state of everyone and everything associated with the time and place, the ancestral house where the rituals take place, rituals of encounter (speeches and chant), visitors who pay respects, the giving of gifts, the commendation of someone who is dying, the farewell speech addressed to the dying just before death and to the dead, the feast which is a rite of reincorporation for the family, the tramping of the deceased person's house to stamp out bad spirits, the unveiling of a memorial (about a year later), the transfer of mourning to another ancestral house by relatives who were unable to be at the funeral. Te Kitohi Pikaahu provided directions on the celebration of funeral liturgies and services in time of death from *A New Zealand Prayer Book,* and the numbers of the pages on which the liturgical material may be found.

Appendix 2

Resources for Funerals

Some Contemporary Anglican Funeral Liturgies

The Anglican Church of Australia (1995), *A Prayer Book for Australia,* Broughton Books, Alexandria NSW.

Brazil: *Livro de Oração Comun* (1987), Oficio de Sepultura, pp. 192–210.

Anglican Church in Canada (1985), *The Book of Alternative Services of the Anglican Church of Canada,* Toronto, Anglican Book Centre, pp. 565–605.

(1992), *Occasional Celebrations,* Toronto, ABC Publishing.

Church of England (2000), *Common Worship: Pastoral Services,* London, Church House Publishing, pp. 214–401.

Church of Ireland (2004), *The Book of Common Prayer,* Dublin, Columba, pp. 465–516.

Anglican Church of Kenya (2002), *Our Modern Services,* Nairobi, Uzima Press.

The Church of Melanesia (1985), *A Melanesian English Prayer Book,* Honiara.

Anglican Church of Nigeria (1996), *The Book of Common Prayer of the Church of Nigeria,* Port Harcourt, CSS Bookshops Ltd.

Church of North India (1995), *The Book of Worship,* New Delhi, ISPCK.

The Anglican Church of Southern Africa, (1989) *An Anglican Prayer Book,* pp. 525–68.

(2008) *Worship Resource file.*

Church of South India (2006), *Book of Common Worship*, CSI Centre, Chennai.

Anglican Church in Thailand (1989), *A Prayer Book for Thailand*, Christ Church Bangkok.

New Zealand (1989), *A New Zealand Prayer Book, He Karakia Mihinare O Aotearoa*, Auckland, Collins, pp. 809–84.

The Scottish Episcopal Church (1987), *Revised Funeral Rites*, Edinburgh.

The Episcopal Church in the United States of America (1979), *The Book of Common Prayer*, pp. 465–507.

(2007) *Enriching our Worship III: Burial Rites for Adults together with a Rite for the Burial of a Child.*

(2007), *Changes: Prayers and Services Honoring Rites of Passage*, pp. 71–8.

Church in Wales (2008), *Proposed Alternative Funeral Rites for the Church in Wales*, Penarth, Church in Wales Publications.

Church in the Province of the West Indies (1995), *Book of Common Prayer*.

Historical Studies

Ariès, Philippe, *The Hour of Our Death*, trans. Helen Weaver. New York, 1981. French ed., *L'homme devant la mort*. Paris, 1977.
Classic work on medieval practices, including domestic practices before and after death.
   Commemorating the Dead: Texts and Artifacts in Context: Studies of Roman, Jewish and Christian Burials. Ed. Laurie Brink & Deborah Green. Berlin & New York, 2008.
Essais sur la mort: Travaux d'un seminaire de recherché sur la mort, ed. Guy Couturier, André Charron, and Guy Durand. Montreal, 1985.
   A rich collection of essays that includes sources such as art and hagiography, in addition to liturgical and domestic texts.
Huntington, Richard & Peter Metcalf, *Celebrations of Death: The Anthropology of Mortuary Ritual*, Cambridge, 1979.
   As the title indicates, an overview of mortuary rituals through the

ages, drawing on religion, culture, geography, climate and other factors.

Kurtz, Donna & John Boardman, *Greek Burial Customs*, Ithaca, 1971.

Lloyd, Trevor, *Funeral Rites*, in *The Oxford Guide to the Book of Common Prayer*, pp. 518–27.

An overview of current funeral rites in the Anglican Communion

Ntedika, Joseph, *L'evocation de l'au-delà dans la prière pour les morts*. Recherches africaine de théologie 2, Louvain, 1971.

A theological study of how liturgical prayer speaks of eternal life in both historical and cultural ways (drawing on several African traditions regarding Christian beliefs and ancestors)

Paxton, Frederick S, *Christianizing Death: The Creation of a Ritual Process in Early Medieval Europe*, Ithaca & London, 1990.

Still one of the best historical overviews of rites for the sick, the dying and the dead in the crucial Western Church period between the sixth and the tenth centuries. Paxton does a fine job of tracing the combining of local traditions into a more centralized body of work under Charlemagne's budget.

Rowell, Geoffrey, *The Liturgy of Christian Burial: An Introductory Survey of the Historical Development of Christian Burial Rites*, London, 1977.

Although slightly dated now, a very helpful survey that carries through from the medieval traditions into the reformation period and beyond, with a particular emphasis on Anglican prayer book trajectories.

Rush, Alfred C., *Death and Burial in Christian Antiquity*. Washington, DC., 1941 (reprinted, 1977).

Also dated, but a good overview of early Christian practices, their similarities and differences with the larger cultures around them. His ancillary article 'The Eucharist: The Sacrament of the Dying in Christian Antiquity' (*Jurist* 34 (1974), pp. 10–35) is still one of the best studies on the roots of *viaticum*.

Sicard, Damien, *La liturgie de la mort dans l'église latine des origins à la réforme carlingienne*. LQF 63. Münster, 1978.

Sicard traces the development of Latin-speaking rites surrounding the dead, with particular attention to North Africa, Spain and Gaul.

Toynbee, J. M. C., *Death and Burial in the Roman World*, Ithaca, 1971.

Dated but helpful in contextualizing early Christian rituals in a wider religious and cultural setting.

Vogel, Cyrille, *Medieval Liturgy: An Introduction to the Sources*. Revised and translated William G. Storey and Niels Krogh Rasumussen. Washington, DC, 1986.

A handy guide to a wealth of medieval liturgical sources, including the *ordines romani* that contain parts of the developing funeral rites.

Theological and Cultural Issues

Becker, Ernest, *The Denial of Death*. New York, 1973.

Becker's work was a classic in North America because he was one of the first popularized voices to challenge the death-avoiding practices in post-WW II America.

Bertman, S. L., *Facing Death: Images, Insights, and Interventions*, New York, 1991.

Bowkey, J, *The Meaning of Death*. Cambridge, 1991.

Davies, Douglas, *Death, Ritual and Belief: The Rhetoric of Funerary Rites*, New York, 2002.

Davies, Douglas, *The Theology of Death*, London, 2007.

Death and Religion in a Changing World, ed. Kathleen Garces-Foley, New York, 2006.

Primarily concerned with North American death practices, but covering Christian and multifaith perspectives by comparison between cultural expressions.

Death Our Future: Christian Theology and Pastoral Practice in Funeral Ministry. Peter C. Jupp, ed., Peterborough, 2008.

Kübler-Ross, E, *On Death and Dying*, London, 1970.

Kübler-Ross, E, *Living with Death and Dying*, London, 1982.

Lampard, John S., *Go Forth, Christian Soul: The Biography of a Prayer*, Peterborough, 2005.

> While primarily a work on Christian dying, Lampard includes changing attitudes toward death between Victorian times and the twentieth century, from the perspective of theology informed by culture.

Pearson, Mike Parker, *The Archeology of Death and Burial*, College Station, 1999.

Pieper, Josef, *Death and Immortality*, London, 1969.

Rahner, Karl, *On the Theology of Death*, (trans. C. Hekey), New York, 1961.

Rites of Death and Dying, ed. Anthony F. Sherman, Collegeville, 1988.

Sheppy, Paul, *Death Liturgy and Ritual: Volume I, A Pastoral and Liturgical Theology*, Aldershot, Hants & Burlington, VT, 2003.

> The first of two volumes deals with issues surrounding funerals and death, such as medicine and the lay, social dimensions of death, and two specifically theological chapters on Christ and death as well as the paschal mystery as lens by which to articulate the meaning of Christian death.

The Oxford Book of Death, D. J. Enright, ed., Oxford, 1983.

White, Vernon, *Life Beyond Death: Threads of Hope in Faith, Life and Theology*, London, 2006.

Woodsmith, Audrey Renee, *The Psychology of Ritual in Anglican Funerals*, GTU Thesis, Berkeley, CA, 2007.

Alternative Rituals and Ecumenical Ritual Resources

Cieslak, William, *Console One Another: Commentary on The Order of Christian Funerals*, Washington, DC, 1990.

> Commentary on the RC rites.

Davies, J. Douglas, *Cremation Today and Tomorrow*, Nottingham, 1990.

Death: A Sourcebook about Christian Death, ed., Virginia Sloyan. Chicago, 1990.

Danals, Cynthia, *Funeral Services*, Nashville, 2007.

Gray, Donald, *Memorial Services*, London, 2002.

Huntington, Richard & Peter Metcalf, *Celebrations of Death: The Anthropology of Mortuary Ritual*, Cambridge, 1976.

Larson-Miller, Lizette, *Scared to Death: Running From our Faith in the Face of Death*, Collegeville, forthcoming, 2012.

Quivik, Melinda, *A Christian Funeral: Witness to the Resurrection*, Minneapolis, 2005.

A Lutheran view of the theological foundations of contemporary funeral practice.

Rutherford, Richard, *Honoring the Dead: Catholics and Cremation Today*, Collegeville, 2001.

Rutherford, Richard & Tony Barr, *The Death of a Christian: The Order of Christian Funerals*, (revised edition), Collegeville, 1990.

After a brief historical overview of funerals, this surveys the new Roman Catholic Funeral and offers pastoral suggestions.

Sheppy, Paul P. J., *Death Liturgy and Ritual: Volume II: A commentary on Liturgical Texts*, Aldershot, Hants & Burlington, VT, 2004.

This second volume looks at how is going on in ecumenically diverse rites, with a long section on Anglican rites, several churches of the reformation, and several uniting churches.

Sheppy, Paul, *In Sure and Certain Hope: Liturgies, Prayers and Readings for Funerals and Memorials*, Norwich, 2003.

FROM THE AUTHORS AND SCM PRESS

Comfortable Words

Polity, Piety and the Book of Common Prayer
Edited by Stephen Platten and Christopher Woods

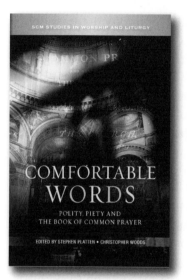

2012 is the 350th anniversary of the 1662 *Book of Common Prayer*, now widely used in the Church of England and throughout the Anglican Communion. *Comfortable Words* draws together some of the world's leading liturgical scholars and historians who offer a comprehensive and accessible study of the Prayer Book and its impact on both Church and society over the last three and a half centuries.

Including new and original scholarship about the use of the *Book of Common Prayer* at different periods during its life, it also sets out some key material on the background to the production of both the Tudor books and the seventeenth-century book itself.

Contributors include some of the leading historians and liturgical scholars of our time, including Bryan Spinks, Paul Bradshaw, William Jacob and Brian Cummings and a Foreword by Diarmaid McCulloch.

978-0-334-04670-7   paperback   200 pp   £45

HOW TO ORDER

Call 01603 785925, email **orders@norwichbooksandmusic.co.uk** or order online at **www.scmpress.co.uk**

Please quote CWJLS02.

UK orders please add £2.50 P&P for orders under £25 or £3.50 for order under £75. Orders over £75 postage free. International orders please call for details.

SCM Press is a division of Hymns Ancient and Modern Ltd, registered charity 270060

The Alcuin Club promotes the study of Christian Liturgy, especially the liturgy of the Anglican Communion. It has a long history of publishing an annual Collection, and has shared with GROW since 1987 in also publishing the Joint Liturgical Studies. Members receive all publications free. For membership contact: The *Alcuin Club*. St Anne's Vicarage, 182 St Ann's Hill, London, SW18 2RS. Telephone; 0208 874 2809. E-mail: gordon,jeanes@stanneswandsworth.org.uk

The Group for Renewal of Worship (GROW) has for 40 years been a focus for forward-thinking, often adventurous, explorations in Anglican worship. It has produced (by its own members writing or by its commissioning of others) over 200 titles in the Grove Worship Series, and until 1986 similarly produced Grove Liturgical Studies, many of which are still in print. Enquiries about GROW to Grove Books Ltd, Ridley Hall Road, Cambridge CB3 9HU, or to members of the Group.

From 1987 to 2004, the Joint Editorial Board of the two sponsoring agencies commissioned numbers1–58 of Joint Liturgical Studies, published by Grove Books Ltd (see the Grove Books website or of previous Joint Liturgical Studies). In 2005, 5CM-Canterbury Press Ltd, now Hymns Ancient & Modern, became the publishers. Two titles (of 48–60 pages) are published each year. Available at £7.95 from Hymns Ancient & Modern.

59 (2005) *Proclus on Baptism in Constantinople* by Juliette Day
60 (2005) *1927–28 Prayer Book Crisis in the Church of England Part 1: Ritual, Royal Commission, and Reply to the Royal Letters of Business* by Donald Gray.
61 (2006) *Prayer Book Crisis...Part 2: The cul-de-sac of the 'Deposited Book'...until further notice be taken* by Donald Gray.
62 (2006) *Anglican Swahili Prayer Books* by Ian Tarrant.
63 (2007) *A History of the International Anglican Liturgical Consultations 1983–2007* by David Holeton and Colin Buchanan.

64 (2007) *Justin Martyr on Baptism and Eucharist* edited by Colin Buchanan

65 (2008) *Anglican Liturgical Identity: Papers from the Prague meeting of the International Anglican Liturgical Consultation* edited by Christopher Irvine

66 (2008) *The Psalms in Christian Worship: Patristic Precedent and Anglican Practice* by Anthony Gelston

67 (2009) *Infant Communion from the Reformation to the Present Day* by Mark Dalby

68 (2009) *The Hampton Court Conference and the 1604 Book of Common Prayer* edited by Colin Buchanan

69 (2010) *Social Science Methods in Contemporary Liturgical Research: An Introduction* by Trevor Lloyd, James Steven and Phillip Tovey

70 (2010) *Two Early Egyptian Liturgical Papyri: The Deir Balyzeh Papyrus and the Barcelona Papyrus* translated and edited by Alistair Stewart

71 (2011) *Anglican Marriage Rites: A symposium* edited by Kenneth W. Stevenson

72 (2011) Charles Simeon on *The Excellency of the Liturgy* by Andrew Atherstone.

73 (2012) Ordo Romanus Primus *Latin Text and Translation with Introduction and Notes* by Alan Griffiths

JLS 75 will be *Admission to C.ommunion: Late Medievals and Reformers* by Mark Dalby..

The current series of Joint Liturgical Studies is available through booksellers, on standing order either by joining the Alcuin Club (see above) or from Hymns Ancient & Modern, Subscription Office, 13a Hellesdon Park Road, Norwich, Norfolk, NR6 5DR, UK. Telephone 01603 785910 or online at www.jointliturgicalstudies.co.uk.

The Alcuin Club
promoting liturgical scholarship and renewal

The Companion to Common Worship (two volumes)
edited by Paul Bradshaw
*a detailed discussion of the origins and development
of each Common Worship rite
together with a comprehensive commentary on the text*
(Volume 1, SPCK 2001 - £19.99)
(Volume 2, SPCK 2006 - £19.99)

Celebrating the Eucharist
by Benjamin Gordon-Taylor & Simon Jones
a practical guide to the celebration of the Eucharist
(SPCK 2005 - £9.99)

The Worship Mall
by Bryan Spinks
*an invitation to walk through the Worship Mall
and see what is on offer in the postmodern culture*
(SPCK 2010 - £14.99)

The Origins of Feasts, Fasts and Seasons
in Early Christianity
by Paul Bradshaw & Maxwell Johnson
*drawing upon the latest research,
this book tracks the development of feasts, fasts and seasons*
(SPCK 2011 - £14.99)

The Eucharistic Liturgies
Their evolution and interpretation
by Paul Bradshaw & Maxwell Johnson
*in this wide ranging study Bradshaw and Johnson examine the origins of the Eucharist and its
use up to our own day.*
(SPCK 2012 - £19.99)

*To order any of these titles, or for details of how to join the Alcuin Club,
email alcuinclub@gmail.com or telephone 01763 248676.
For all full list of Alcuin titles, go to www.alcuinclub.org.uk
Generous discounts available to members.*